20 BEST SALTWATER AQUARIUM FISH (SPECIES GUIDE FOR BEGINNERS)

With hundreds, if not thousands of marine fish in the trade, choosing the best saltwater fish for beginners was a real challenge!

Here are the main criteria I used to decide on which were the best saltwater fish for beginners:

- **Inexpensive:** Most of the saltwater fish here on the inexpensive side of the trade. The Four Stripe Damselfish may be the best value and can be found for as little as $4.99 in stores.

- Adult Flame Angelfish and Black Cap Basslets can set you back $45-60 but are still relatively inexpensive, as marine fish run.
- Hardy: Marine fish can be notoriously difficult to feed or provide good water quality for. Many are sensitive to temperature, salinity, or pH swings. While a few are picky eaters (many Angelfish and Tangs) the majority will accept a wide variety of prepared and frozen offerings and are not especially sensitive to water conditions so long as they are stable and clean.
- Small to Medium Sized: Beginner saltwater aquarists are rarely buying 300+ gallon setups. And unfortunately, many of the most commonly seen marine fish in the trade will outgrow your average tank. Each one of the fish I chose below will do well in aquariums ranging from 10 to 100 gallons in volume.

Keep in mind that other criteria such as aggressiveness, reef-safety, activity level, or a predatory nature may disqualify a particular fish from your aquarium plans.

DAMSELFISH

Damselfish are very often one of the first first that new saltwater aquarium owners purchase. This section dives into a few common damselfish species:

Beginner saltwater aquarists looking for their "Nemo" have come to the right place. There are actually two species of clownfish to look at; the Ocellaris or Common Ocellaris Clownfish, and A. percula, the Percula Clownfish.

Both look nearly identical, however the Common Clownfish has thinner black lines, 11 dorsal fin spines, and more dark pigmentation in the eyes. Percula Clownfish are smaller, more expensive and more sensitive to poor water conditions, making them ideal for intermediate to advanced hobbyists.

Anemones are half the fun of keeping Clownfish. Due to a mutually symbiotic arrangement, Clownfish nestle among the stinging tentacles of the anemone for protection. In exchange the Clownfish will drop bits of food directly onto its mouth and defend it from potential predators.

However, Common Clownfish need not be kept with anemones. Anemones have specialized needs in terms of water quality and lighting that are challenging and expensive for beginners to replicate.

Instead, Common Clownfish will thrive in saltwater fish-only community tanks of at least 20 gallons with peaceful species and plenty of live rock to dart in and out of. They are active, hardy carnivores and will accept a wide range of prepared foods mixed with meaty frozen and live items.

- **Scientific Name:** Amphiprion ocellaris
- **Length:** 3-4 inches
- **Temperament:** Peaceful
- **Aquarium Size:** 20 gallons
- **Reef Safe:** Yes

These Caribbean Damselfish are an intense, iridescent blue and need to be kept in schools of around 6 individuals. Damselfish of all kinds are hardy, eager feeders, and some of the best saltwater fish for beginners. Chromis in particular are a great choice because they are less aggressive compared to most of their Clownfish and DASCYLLUS sp. cousins.

Blue Reef Chromis tend to hang in the middle to upper water column, near prominent coral outgrowths.

As zooplankton feeders they prefer to pick out smaller food particles from the water as it flows by – a surface to mid level powerhead gives them current to swim against and dart into for food

Like most upper water zooplankton feeders Blue Reef Chromis are reef-safe and won't pick at corals or invertebrates. This habit makes them ideal dither fish for the saltwater aquarium because they help shy fish feel at ease.

Chromis Damselfish as a whole are hardy, inexpensive, and are often some of the first fish introduced to a cycling aquarium. While unaggressive, they will set up a pecking order amongst themselves. So long as they are kept in moderately sized groups no one member will be harassed to death.

- **Scientific Name:** Chromis cyaneus
- **Length:** 4 to 5 inches
- **Temperament:** Peaceful, Schooling
- **Aquarium Size:** 30 gallons
- **Reef Safe:** Yes

Four Stripe Damselfish are some of the best saltwater fish for beginners – but are also not without their challenges! Specifically, they are quite aggressive and territorial as they grow older, both towards their own kind and other species.

On the plus side, they have a bold black and silver pattern that's eye catching and are extremely hardy in terms of water quality shifts. Four Stripe Damselfish will accept any sort of carnivorous food offering and are also reef-safe, offering a stark color contrast to the pinks, greens, and purples of coral and live rock.

Four Stripe Damselfish will usually claim a rocky outcropping as their territory and will viciously nip at any intruders. When kept in tanks smaller than 30 gallons this territory can extend to most of the aquarium, and can end in tank mate deaths due to stress.

Instead of pairing these aggressive little fish with peaceful tank mates, choose similar sized to larger fish that are on the semi-aggressive spectrum yet can't actually eat them. Angelfish, smaller Triggerfish, and Wrasses are a good match both in size and temperament.

Interestingly, all Four Stripe Damselfish are female unless kept in groups. Through social dynamics dominant fish eventually become males and will court the other females of his new harem!

- **Scientific Name:** Dascyllus melanurus
- **Length:** 3-4 inches
- **Temperament:** Aggressive, Territorial
- **Aquarium Size:** 30 Gallons
- **Reef Safe:** Yes

- Damselfish are active, often aggressive fish that tend to stake out territories and defend them vigorously.
- Many Clownfish and Chromis are gentler and peaceful while larger Clownfish and Dascyllus Damselfish tend to be the most aggressive.
- Damselfish are very hardy when it comes to water quality and will accept nearly any prepared or frozen food items.

ANGELFISH

Saltwater Angelfish are, undoubtedly, one of the most attractive groups of saltwater aquarium fish. This section dives into a few species of Angelfish that you can keep at home.

Flame Angelfish are not only intensely colored but are smaller, less specialized, and easier to care for than their larger cousins. They are great saltwater fish for beginners because they feed mostly on algae and occasionally invertebrates. Many of their larger cousins feed almost exclusively on sponges, which gets expensive quickly. Flame Angelfish will take vegetarian flake offerings mixed with occasional snacks of protein rich flakes or frozen items.

While Flame Angelfish are hardy as Angelfish go they should be some of the last fish to introduce to your new saltwater aquarium.

Once the tank is mostly cycled you will have little trouble with them. They are also peaceful as far as Angelfish go – Flame Angelfish may claim a small territory but aren't nearly as aggressive as other species.

Unfortunately, no Angelfish is truly reef-safe. Nearly all species are grazers of live rock, feeding on algae, bryozoans, sponges, and corals. Flame Angelfish are mostly algae feeders and are one of the best Angelfish to consider for a reef aquarium. However there's always a chance of one taking a liking to a soft coral or clam mantle.

- **Scientific Name:** Centropyge loriculus
- **Length:** 3 to 4 inches
- **Temperament:** Peaceful, occasionally Territorial
- **Aquarium Size:** 20+ Gallons
- **Reef Safe:** Somewhat

Bicolor Angelfish are some of the largest of the Centropyge Dwarf Angelfish, reaching almost 6 inches in length. They are also on the more aggressive end, particularly towards other Angelfish. However, you can minimize their aggressiveness by providing a spacious tank with plenty of live rock outcroppings to break line of sight and establish a territory.

Like most omnivorous Angelfish species Bicolors are easy to feed but are not reef-safe because they graze continually and will find many sessile invertebrates tempting. Bicolor Angelfish are inexpensive and easy to find however are a little on the sensitive side in terms of water quality.

The tank should be allowed to fully cycle and they should be the last fish added.

- **Scientific Name:** Centropyge bicolor
- **Length:** Up to 6 inches
- **Temperament:** Semi-aggressive
- **Aquarium Size:** 55 Gallons
- **Reef Safe:** No

Rock Beauty Angelfish are a good saltwater fish for beginners if you're looking for a larger species. Reaching up to 10 inches in length, these Atlantic Holacanthus Angelfish are specialist sponge feeders. This means you'll need to purchase large quantities of frozen marine Angelfish preparation, mixed with Spirulina flakes and frozen meaty fare.

Choosing tankmates for them can be a bother because Rock Beauties are semi-aggressive but have no tolerance for aggressive tank mates. Fast swimming, peaceful tank mates like Blue Reef Chromis, Tangs, and bottom dwellers like Gobies are great additions.

So long as they are properly fed and their tank mates are on the passive side, Rock Beauty Angelfish are hardy in terms of water quality and are impressively large without being true tank busters.

- **Scientific Name:** Holacanthus tricolor
- **Length:** Up to 10 inches
- **Temperament:** Semi-aggressive
- **Aquarium Size:** 70 Gallons
- **Reef Safe:** No

- Angelfish tend to have specialized diets high in either algae or sponges that need to be accounted for.
- Even the most peaceful Angelfish tend to be territorial of both each other and other fish and should be given space for territories and breaks in line of sight.
- Angelfish are on the sensitive side and should be the last fish to add to an aquarium in the process of being cycled.

TANGS

Tangs are popular for their bright colors are unique traits, but they can be a bit more challanging than the other species on our list.

If you already have a bit of experience with saltwater fish-keeping, here are a few tang species that you should look into:

Yellow Tangs are bright lemon colored vegetarians that are reef safe and provide a service by browsing continually on filamentous algae that competes with corals and anemones for light and nutrients.

When purchased young, Yellow Tangs can even be raised in groups that will naturally form a school as they mature. They are also entirely peaceful and won't both tank mates. However, you should be aware that aggressive tank mates may find Surgeonfish problematic.

They get their name from a retractable jackknife-like barb along the tail.

When threatened Tangs and Surgeonfish flick this barb at their assailants, opening up deep gashes that can lead to infection.

While fairly hardy, Yellow Tangs are sometimes the canary in the coal mine when water quality drops. Tangs and Surgeonfish are particularly prone to Head and Lateral Line Erosion Disease (HLLE), also known as "Hole in the Head."

Under no circumstances should you buy a Tang in the store displaying gouges of missing skin or flesh along the lateral line. While the causes are not entirely known, poor nutrition and water quality are thought to be the main reasons. Vitamin C (found in vegetable matter) is also thought to alleviate the disease.

- **Scientific Name:** Zebrasoma flavescens
- **Length:** Up to 8 inches
- **Temperament:** Peaceful
- **Aquarium Size:** 55 Gallons
- **Reef Safe:** Yes

Also known as the Hippo Tang or Blue Surgeonfish, Blue Tangs are the Dory to your Nemo. They are midwater dwelling species that eat a fair amount of zooplankton as well as the usual algae and seaweed that all Tangs love. Offer them Mysis and Brine Shrimp in addition to vegetarian fare for best health and color.

Blue Tangs are active and peaceful towards other fish but aggressive and intolerant of both their own kind and other Tangs. They are also larger Tangs, reaching up to 12 inches in length. So long as your tank can accommodate one, they are impressively large, reef-safe inhabitants.

Like all Tangs and Surgeonfish, Powder Blue Tangs may show symptoms of HLLE if fed standard animal-based fish food. Offer a diverse range of seaweed, Spirulina flakes, and even blanched vegetables like Cauliflower and Spinach to ensure they get enough vitamins.

- **Scientific Name:** Paracanthurus hepatus
- **Length:** 10 to 12 inches
- **Temperament:** Peaceful to Semi-aggressive
- **Aquarium Size:** 100 Gallons
- **Reef Safe:** Yes

Kole Tangs are an especially great addition to reef tanks with algae issues because they eat a wide range of types, including brown diatomaceous algae. While often considered herbivores Kole Tangs are better classified as "detritivores."

They feed on the debris within and coating live rocks, consuming algae, tiny invertebrates, diatoms, protozoans, and other minute creatures that normally coat any surface in a mature aquarium. Kole Tangs will even graze on aquarium glass and equipment, helping to keep your tank looking spotless.

Kole Tangs are especially gentle and can even be kept with other Tangs – however, you'll want to keep a close eye on them both because other Tangs are rarely so forgiving. When paired with gentler species that feed on different algae species like Yellow Tangs, they form an algae-busting duo that's hard to match.

- **Scientific Name:** Ctenochaetus strigosus
- **Length:** 7 inches
- **Temperament:** Peaceful
- **Aquarium Size:** 70 Gallons
- **Reef Safe:** Yes

GENERAL TANG NOTES

- Tangs prefer moderate current, especially Blue Tangs.
- Tangs are mostly vegetarian and need vegetable matter to avoid diseases due to vitamin deficiencies.
- While intolerant of each other Tangs are generally peaceful, reef-safe fish. Watch for their retractable tail blades that they will use both against aggressive tank mates and when netted!

BASS AND BASSLETS

In this section we discuss a few unique bass and basslet species:

The Chalk Bass is an often overlooked choice that is one of the best saltwater fish for beginners! As its name suggests, it's actually in the same family as Sea Bass and even the Giant Grouper, one of the largest bony fish in existence!

Chalk Bass are predators however they only feed on zooplankton, tiny invertebrates, fish fry, and other small prey items. Maxing out at 2 to 3 inches in length, they are excellent community tank dwellers and even reef-safe, though you should be careful of keeping them with the smallest of reef shrimp. Even tiny crabs are far too crunchy to be a meal for Chalk Bass.

These dwarf Bass are also sociable, forming small shoals in the wild. Allow for 10 gallons of space per Chalk Bass you intend to keep. Individually, they make great nano-reef inhabitants. Their relatively unflashy colors and abundance in North American Atlantic waters makes them inexpensive and easy to obtain.

When first introduced, Chalk Bass tend to be quite shy and will stay hidden but dither fish, ample hiding places, and treats of live and frozen food will soon encourage them to stay out in the open. Chalk Bass are hardy, peaceful, and overall one of the best saltwater fish for beginners!

- **Scientific Name:** Serranus tortugarum
- **Length:** 2 to 3 inches
- **Temperament:** Peaceful
- **Aquarium Size:** 10 gallons
- **Reef Safe:** Yes

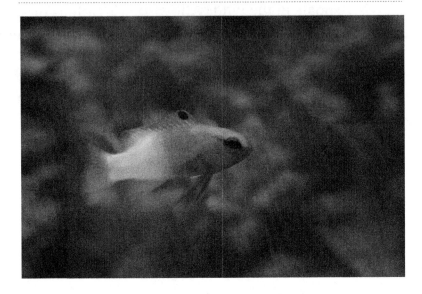

Royal Gramma are iconic saltwater fish seen regularly in the pet trade. These Caribbean Basslets are hardy, easy to feed, and very inexpensive. They stay small, maxing out at around 3 inches, and are zooplankton feeders in nature.

Royal Gramma are entirely peaceful but should absolutely be kept singly in all but the largest of aquariums and be given a small cave. Like most Basslets they will claim a small hollow and defend it vigorously from intruders. Aquariums with lots of live rock that forms nooks and crannies is best. They will dart from their chosen cave to snap up Brine Shrimp, Bloodworms, and floating prepared foods before quickly returning home.

So long as other fish don't try to push them out Royal Grammas are model community citizens but overly curious tank mates may suffer a nip or chase on occasion. Unfortunately they are also entirely intolerant of other Royal Gramma unless kept in large tanks (55+ gallons) where they can claim caves without seeing each other often.

In especially large aquariums (100+ gallons) you can try keeping a harem. Like many saltwater fish, Royal Gramma are all female until social dynamics induces the dominant fish to become a male. Males are not only larger but even more intensely colored!

- **Scientific Name:** Gramma loreto
- **Length:** 2 to 3 inches
- **Temperament:** Peaceful; Territorial
- **Aquarium Size:** 20 Gallons
- **Reef Safe:** Yes

The Black Cap Basslet is a slightly larger close cousin of the Royal Gramma. It is a little rarer in the aquarium trade as it is found in slightly deeper waters. This drives the price up somewhat but rarely over $50.

Black Cap Basslets have identical care requirements to the Royal Gramma and are just as hardy. The intensely purple coloration with deeper purple forehead is truly remarkable and just as eye-catching as the Royal Gramma's half and half coloration.

Being slightly larger than Royal Gramma, be certain any reef invertebrates aren't tiny enough to be consumed, otherwise it is an excellent reef inhabitant.

- **Scientific Name:** Gramma melacara
- **Length:** 3 to 4 inches
- **Temperament:** Peaceful; Territorial
- **Aquarium Size:** 30 Gallons
- **Reef Safe:** Yes

- While carnivorous Dwarf Bass and Basslets feel mostly on zooplankton and tiny invertebrates, making them safe additions to any fish aquarium.
- Bass and Basslets are reef-safe and won't molest larger invertebrates.
- Chalk Bass are sociable and schooling but Basslets are territorial and will fight one another in smaller aquaria. There are several available species of Dwarf Bass in the trade so do your research. Some species (like the Harlequin Bass – Serranus tigrinus) eventually grow fairly large and are solitary, semi-aggressive predators.

OTHER GREAT SALTWATER AQUARIUM FISH

Here are a few other saltwater fish species that you should consider when setting up your tank:

Also known as the Firefish or Magnificent Dartfish, these are one of the more striking saltwater fish for beginners. Found in the Indopacific region from East Africa all the way to Hawaii, Dartfish get their name from their habit of instantly darting to cover among rubble and coral when threatened.

Fire Gobies are planktivores, feeding on floating plankton and crustaceans that waft by their chosen burrows. They have similar behavior patterns to Basslets in that they will claim a hiding place and hover around the immediate area, only leaving to feed but quickly returning if feeling exposed.

Baby and adult Brine Shrimp and similarly sized frozen items along with prepared flake and pellets are eagerly accepted.

Unlike some cave dwellers Fire Gobies are not territorial and can easily be bullied from their chosen hiding place. If kept with other cave dwellers like Basslets you should ensure there are plenty of places for hiding in case the Fire Gobies get kicked out. Fire Gobies are territorial towards one another and should only be kept together in tanks larger than 55 gallons.

- **Scientific Name:** Nemateleotris magnifica
- **Length:** Up to 3 inches
- **Temperament:** Peaceful
- **Aquarium Size:** 20 Gallons
- **Reef Safe:** Yes

Cardinalfish are unusual looking, strikingly patterned schooling fish found throughout the Western Pacific Ocean. Pajama Cardinalfish are some of the most unusual looking of all, with their huge red eyes, black strike, and polka dot rear half.

Many species of Cardinalfish, including this one, school together among the spines of sea urchins, particularly the long-spined venomous Diadema species. Unlike Clownfish the Cardinalfish offer no benefit to the Sea Urchin and are probably not even noticed, but cause it no harm, either.

In the aquarium Cardinalfish as a whole are some of the best saltwater fish for beginners. While initially shy and reluctant feeders they can be tempted with live and frozen foods and eventually weaned onto prepared foods. When kept in schools they become far more personable and bold, swimming in open water and occasionally displaying to one another.

Other Cardinalfish that are great for beginners include the Banggaii Cardinalfish (Pterapogon kauderni) and Flame Cardinalfish (Apogon maculatus). Both are also schooling, peaceful community dwellers that max out at around 3 inches in length.

- **Scientific Name:** Sphaeramia nematoptera
- **Length:** 3 inches
- **Temperament:** Peaceful; Schooling
- **Aquarium Size:** 20 Gallons
- **Reef Safe:** Yes

Longnose Hawkfish are incredibly unusual saltwater fish found across the Indopacific region. Rather than swim around actively they perch on rock and coral outcroppings waiting for small fish and invertebrates to wander too close, hence the name "Hawkfish."

While predatory and willing to consume especially small tank mates Longnose Hawkfish have tiny mouths and aren't a threat to similarly sized fish and large invertebrates. They are territorial however, choosing a perch and chasing fish away with similar habits like Flame Hawkfish, Gobies, and other sedentary fish.

Longnose Hawkfish are somewhat reef safe and need to be carefully considered. Their perching habits can make them irritating to corals, however, causing them to close up whenever the Longnose Hawkfish decides to sit. They may also receive strings from anemones on occasion when trying to find a spot to perch. Also, smaller shrimp are some of their favorite prey items.

- **Scientific Name:** Oxycirrhites typus
- **Length:** Up to 5 inches
- **Temperament:** Predatory; Territorial
- **Aquarium Size:** 55 Gallons
- **Reef Safe:** With Caution

Lionfish (Pteros sp.) are elegant, graceful Scorpionfish (Scorpaenidae) with a hearty appetite. However most of the larger species require especially large tanks and have a bad habit of eating their tank mates along the way.

Dwarf Lionfish actually describes two particular species; the Shortfin or Fuzzy Lionfish (Dendrochirus brachypterus) and the Fu Manchu Lionfish (Dendrochirus biocellatus). Like their larger cousins they have venomous dorsal spines they won't hesitate to use when feeling threatened.

While rarely needing medical attention the wound is excruciatingly painful – running the wound under water as hot as you can stand breaks down the venom.

As active predators getting them to feed can be a bit of a challenge, especially when first introduced to a new aquarium. Providing meaty items on a feeding stick that dangle and twist in the water like squid and worms will encourage a feeding response. Over time they can be trained onto fresh and frozen items.

While they ignore corals and are reef safe, Dwarf Lionfish really aren't invertebrate safe. They will gladly gulp down shrimp and other mobile invertebrates. And their mouths are a good deal larger than you might expect. It's best not to keep even large shrimp with Dwarf Lionfish as they won't survive the Lionfish trying and failing to consume them.

Keep in mind this also applies to smaller fish –
anything half their size or under is likely to be
eaten. Fish close to their size will be ignored,
however.

- **Scientific Name:** Dendrochirus
  brachypterus and D. biocellatus
- **Length:** 4 to 5 inches
- **Temperament:** Predatory
- **Aquarium Size:** 30 Gallons
- **Reef Safe:** With Caution

Butterfly fish as a whole tend to be picky, sensitive fish. However the Threadfin Butterflyfish is an exception to the family and are the best Butterflyfish for beginners. Found across the Indopacific region, Butterflyfish are close relatives of marine Angelfish and have very similar habits.

Butterflyfish are grazers, picking on corals, algae, polyps, and even tiny anemones. As a result they are not reef-safe but do well in fish only aquariums. Threadfin Butterflyfish are peaceful and non-territorial but will chase their own kind and similar looking fish.

Unlike Angelfish, Threadfin Butterflyfish don't eat much algae and should be offered more meaty fare. They are eager eaters and bold open water swimmers, readily greeting anyone who approaches the tank. Their bold nature and peaceful disposition often encourages shy community dwellers to come out into the open.

- **Scientific Name:** Chaetodon auriga
- **Length:** 8 inches
- **Temperament:** Peaceful
- **Aquarium Size:** 70 gallons
- **Reef Safe:** No

Printed in Great Britain
by Amazon

38019330R00030